Pocket Prayer Book

Compiled by
John O'Holohan, SJ

CHARIS

Servant Publications
Ann Arbor, Michigan

Copyright © 1988 John O'Holohan, S.J.

This edition in the United States of America
is published by
Servant Publications
P.O. Box 8617
Ann Arbor, Michigan 48107

This book was first published under the title of
My Pocket Prayer Book by Veritas Publications in 1988
7-8 Lower Abbey Street
Dublin 1
Ireland

Imprimatur: Adrian Mung'andu,
                archbishop of Lusaka

Cover design by Gerald Gawronski/The Look

93 94 95 96 97 10 9 8 7 6 5 4 3 2 1

Printed in the United States of America
ISBN 0-89283-837-X

Library of Congress Cataloging-in-Publication Data

My pocket prayer book.
Pocket prayer book: selections / by John O'Holohan.—
[1st American ed.]
    96p. cm
Originally published: My pocket prayer book. Dublin :
Veritas Publications, 1988.
    ISBN 0-89283-837-X
    1. Catholic Church—Prayer-books and devotions—
English. I. O'Holohan, John.   II. Title
    BX2182.2.M9   1993
    242'.2—dc20   93-3786

Contents

Introduction

Jesus said, 'All that my Father has is mine; that is why I said that the Spirit will take what I give Him and tell it to you' *(Jn. 16:15)*. The great teacher of prayer is God. His Spirit is always helping us to pray, but this little book can help to bring back our distracted minds to Him. It can help private and family prayer. It is meant to help and guide you through Christian life.

The first Irish edition of *Pocket Prayer Book* was printed in 1971. Five more editions followed and now you have the seventh edition, revised and enlarged. This is the first American edition of the book. It comprises three features in one book – Prayers, Sacraments, and Doctrine. 'We ask God to fill you with the knowledge of his will, with all the wisdom and the understanding that his Spirit gives' *(Col. 1:9)*.

John O'Holohan, SJ

Section 1
PRAYER

'Lord, teach us to pray.' (*Luke 11:1*)

PART 1 — MOST USEFUL PRAYERS
(*for memorising*)

1. Sign of the Cross (*in memory of Redemption and Trinity*)
2. Our Father (*given to us by Jesus himself*)
3. Hail Mary (*first half by Angel Gabriel*)
4. Glory be to the Father (*in honour of Blessed Trinity*)
5. Morning Offering (*makes our life a prayer*)
6. Guardian Angel (*asks help of guarding angels*)
7. Act of Contrition (*gains God's pardon and love*)
8. Apostles' Creed (*our profession of Faith*)
9. Hail Holy Queen (*brings us to Jesus*)
10. Holy Spirit (*makes us holy and united in Christ*)

1. ✠ Sign of the Cross
In the name of the Father and of the Son and of the Holy Spirit, Amen.

2. Our Father
Our Father, who art in heaven, hallowed be thy name,

6

thy kingdom come, thy will be done on earth as it is in heaven. Give us this day our daily bread, and forgive us our trespasses, as we forgive them that trespass against us. And lead us not into temptation, but deliver us from evil. Amen.

3. Hail Mary

Hail Mary, full of grace, the Lord is with thee: blessed art thou among women, and blessed is the fruit of thy womb, Jesus. Holy Mary, Mother of God, pray for us sinners, now, and at the hour of our death. Amen.

4. Glory be to the Father

Glory be to the Father, and to the Son, and to the Holy Spirit, as it was in the beginning, is now, and ever shall be, world without end. Amen.

5. The Morning Offering of the Apostleship of Prayer

O Jesus, through the most pure heart of Mary, I offer you all my prayers, works, joys and sufferings of this day for all the intentions of your Divine Heart.

6. My Guardian Angel

Angel of God, my guardian dear, to whom God's love entrusts me here, ever this day be at my side, to light and guard, to rule and guide.

7. Act of Contrition

O my God, because you are so good, I am very sorry that I have sinned against you, and with the help of your grace I will not sin again.

8. Apostles' Creed

I believe in God, the Father almighty,
creator of heaven and earth.
I believe in Jesus Christ, his only son, our Lord.
He was conceived by the power of the Holy Spirit
and born of the Virgin Mary.
He suffered under Pontius Pilate
was crucified, died and was buried.
He descended to the dead.
On the third day he rose again.
He ascended into heaven,
and is seated at the right hand of the Father.
He will come to judge the living and the dead.
I believe in the Holy Spirit, the Holy Catholic Church,
the communion of saints, the forgiveness of sins,
the resurrection of the body, and life everlasting.
Amen.

9. The Hail Holy Queen (*Salve Regina*)

Hail, holy Queen, mother of mercy; hail our life, our sweetness, and our hope! To you do we cry, poor banished children of Eve; to you do we send up our sighs, mourning and weeping in this vale of tears. Turn then, most gracious advocate, your eyes of mercy towards us; and after this our exile, show to us the blessed fruit of your womb, Jesus.

O clement, O loving, O sweet Virgin Mary.
V. Pray for us, O holy Mother of God.
R. That we may be made worthy of the promises of Christ.

10. Come Holy Spirit!

Come Holy Spirit, fill the hearts of your faithful and kindle in them the fire of your love.
Send forth your spirit
And they shall be created
And you will renew the face of the earth.

Let us pray:
O God, who has taught the hearts of the faithful by the light of the Holy Spirit, grant that by the gift of the same Spirit we may be always truly wise and ever rejoice in his consolation, through Christ Our Lord, Amen.

PART 2 — MORE USEFUL PRAYERS

11. Act of Faith

My God, I believe that you are the one God in three divine persons, Father, Son and Holy Spirit. I believe all that you teach through your Church because your word is true.

12. Act of Hope

My God, in trust in your goodness and promises. I hope to be forgiven my sins, to be helped by you and to be taken to heaven through the power and goodness of Jesus Christ, my Lord and Saviour.

13. Act of Love

My God, I love you above all things with all my mind and heart because you are so good. For your sake I love other people as I love myself.

14. **Before meals**

Dear God, our Father, please bless both those who have prepared this food and those who are going to eat it. We make this prayer to you through your son, Jesus Christ, our Lord. Amen.

15. **After meals**

Thank you, Lord, for your gift to us of the food we have eaten and enjoyed. May our sharing of this meal keep us always united in Christ Jesus, your son. Amen.

16. **The Angelus**

May be said morning, noon, and night, to put us in mind that God the Son became man for our salvation.

V. The Angel of the Lord declared unto Mary:
R. And she conceived of the Holy Spirit.
    Hail Mary, etc.
V. Behold the handmaid of the Lord:
R. Be it done unto me according to your word.
    Hail Mary, etc.
V. And the Word was made Flesh:
R. And dwelt among us.
    Hail Mary, etc.
V. Pray for us, O holy Mother of God.
R. That we may be made worthy of the promises of Christ.

Let us pray:
Pour forth, we beseech you, O Lord, your grace into our hearts, that we, to whom the incarnation of Christ, your son, was made known by the message of an angel, may be brought by his passion and cross to the glory

of his resurrection, through the same Christ our Lord.
R. Amen.

May the divine assistance remain always with us and
may the souls of the faithful departed, through the
mercy of God, rest in peace.
R. Amen.

17. **O Queen of Heaven** (*Regina Coeli*)
   for Easter Season
O Queen of heaven, rejoice! Alleluia.
For he whom you did merit to bear, Alleluia,
Has risen as he said. Alleluia.
Pray for us to God. Alleluia.

V. Rejoice and be glad, O Virgin Mary, Alleluia,
R. For the Lord has risen indeed. Alleluia.

Let us pray:
O God, who gave joy to the world through the
resurrection of your son our Lord Jesus Christ, grant
that we may obtain, through his Virgin Mother, Mary,
the joys of everlasting life. Through the same Christ
our Lord.
R. Amen.

18. **En Ego** (*Prayer before a Crucifix*)
Behold, O good and most sweet Jesus, I cast myself
upon my knees in your sight, and with the most fervent
desire of my soul I pray and beseech you to impress
upon my heart lively sentiments of faith, hope and
charity, with true repentance for my sins and a most
firm desire of amendment: whilst with deep affection
and grief of soul I consider within myself and mentally

contemplate your five most precious wounds, having before my eyes that which David, the prophet, long ago spoke in your person concerning you, O good Jesus: They have pierced my hands and my feet; they have numbered all my bones.

19. Prayer to Christ, King of All

O Christ Jesus! I acknowledge you as King of All. Whatever has been made has been created for you. Exercise your rights over me.

I renew my baptismal promises, renouncing Satan with all his works and vanities, and promising to live as a good Christian. I pledge myself to promote, as far as in me lies, the triumph of God's rights and those of your Church.

Divine Heart of Jesus, I offer you my feeble help to make all hearts recognise your Sacred Kingship and thus to establish the reign of peace in the world. Amen.

20. Memorare

Remember, O most loving Virgin Mary, that it is a thing unheard of, that anyone ever had recourse to your protection, implored your help, or sought your intercession, and was left forsaken. Filled therefore with confidence in your goodness I fly to you, O Mother, Virgin of Virgins. To you I come, before you I stand, a sorrowful sinner. Despise not my poor words, O Mother of the Word of God, but graciously hear and grant my prayer. (*St Bernard, 1091-1153*)

21. Prayer for studies

O Lord God, fount of wisdom, and source of all true

knowledge, enlighten our minds with the brightness of your truth; drive far from us the darkness of ignorance and error. Give us, Lord, keen understanding and a good memory for what we have understood. Make us willing to learn, and eager to study.

Be with us at our work — direct its progress and help in its completion. Through Christ our Lord. Amen.

22. Prayer for the choice of a career

O Lord, let me know clearly the work you are calling me to do in life. Give me every help I need to answer your call with courage and love and lasting dedication to your will. We ask you also kindly to give many young people the grace of vocation to become priests, brothers and sisters so that your Gospel may be preached and practised everywhere.

23. Prayer for generosity

Dearest Lord Jesus, teach me to be generous, teach me to love and serve you as you deserve, to give and not to count the cost, to fight and not to mind the wounds, to work and not to seek for rest, to labour and to look for no reward except that I do your Holy Will. Amen. (*St Ignatius Loyola, 1491-1556*)

24. Self-dedication to Christ

Take, O Lord, and receive all my liberty, my memory, my understanding, my will. All that I have and possess you have given to me. I restore it all to you. I surrender it in order that you may dispose of it according to your will. Only give me your love and your grace and I am rich enough and desire nothing more. *(St Ignatius Loyola)*

25. Heroic Offering of the Pioneer Total Abstinence Association

For your greater glory and consolation, O Sacred Heart of Jesus, for your sake to give good example, to practise self-denial, to make reparation to you for the sins of intemperance and for the conversion of excessive drinkers I will abstain for life from all intoxicating drink. Amen.

26. An instrument of your peace

Lord, make me an instrument of your peace.
Where there is hatred, let me sow love;
Where there is injury, let me sow pardon;
Where there is doubt, let me sow faith;
Where there is despair, let me give hope;
Where there is darkness, let me give light;
Where there is sadness, let me give joy.

O Divine Master, grant that I may
not try to be comforted, but to comfort;
not try to be understood, but to understand;
not try to be loved, but to love;
because it is in giving that we receive,
it is in forgiving that we are forgiven,
and it is in dying that we are born into eternal life.
Amen. *(St Francis of Assisi, 1181-1226)*

27. For the sick

O Lord Jesus, when you were on earth you had pity on the sick and cured their diseases. Hear our prayer

now, as we ask you to give your merciful help to ....
who is sick. Give him/her good health so that he/she
may live to praise you and to serve you. Amen.

28. In the presence of the dead

We commend to you, O Lord, the soul of your servant
.... Dead to the world, may he/she find life with
you. In your merciful goodness forgive the sins he/she
has committed in this life through human weakness.
Through Christ our Lord. Amen.

29. Prayer for our country

O God, the Father of all the people of the earth, look
with favour on us, and hear the prayer we make for
our country.
Bless all the people of our land — deliver us from evil.
Heal our misunderstandings — and teach us to love
one another.
Give wisdom to our rulers — and a spirit of loyalty
and obedience to all our people.
We ask your fatherly guidance especially for our young
men and women, upon whom the future depends.
Guide the work of our hands and the decisions of our
leaders so that our country may deserve an honoured
place among the nations. Amen.

30. For the local Church

Father, in each and every local church, pilgrims here
on earth, you show forth your one, holy, catholic and
apostolic Church. Gathered around its shepherd may
this family grow in the love and unity of the Holy Spirit
through the Gospel and the Eucharist in the world,
through Christ Our Lord, Amen.

31. For the unity of Christians

God our Father, bring the hearts of all believers together in praise of you and in seeking renewal and reconciliation. May the divisions between Christians be overcome. Make us one in faith and love as we walk with Christ to the joy of your eternal kingdom, through the same Christ Our Lord. Amen.

'He who prays will be saved,
He who does not pray will be lost.'
(*St Alphonsus Ligouri, 1696-1787*)

PART 3 — MORNING PRAYERS

'Very early the next morning. . . Jesus got up. . . went. . . prayed.' (*Mk. 1:35*). A new day has come, a gift from God our Father. Let us thank him. *You could say some or all of these prayers as you begin your day.*

In the name of the Father and of the Son and of the Holy Spirit, Amen.

O Jesus through the most pure heart of Mary, I offer you the prayers, works, joys and sufferings of this day, for all the intentions of your Divine Heart.

Heavenly Father I thank you for keeping me safe during the night which has passed, and for giving me another day in which to serve you; you have created me, redeemed me through your Son, Jesus Christ, and called me to your eternal kingdom; therefore, I want to belong to you completely today, for the rest of my life, and for all eternity. May your holy will be done in me. Give me light that I may know what I ought to do for you this day. Protect me from all evil; lead me through your son Jesus Christ: fill me with the love of the Holy Spirit; I wish to do all for your glory and through love of you.

Our Father, who art in heaven, etc. — *of section 1, N.2*
Hail Mary, full of grace, etc. — *S.1.N.3*
I believe in God the Father Almighty, creator of heaven and earth, etc. — *S.1.N.8*

PART 4 — PRAYERS DURING THE DAY

Jesus told us, 'You must pray always' *(Lk. 18:1)*. St Paul urges us, 'Pray on every occasion, as the Spirit leads' *(Eph. 6:18)*.

Short prayers during the day
Would it not be well to say a little word to God from time to time during the day, to show that you are thinking of him?

Here are a few occasions:

— *before beginning your work, make the Sign of the Cross:*
    In the Name of the Father and of the Son and of the Holy Spirit. Amen.

— *in passing near a church:*
Blessed be Jesus Christ in the Holy Sacrament.

— *on seeing a crucifix:*
We adore you, O Jesus, and we bless you, because by your Holy Cross you have redeemed the world.

— *before beginning your prayers and your lessons:*
Come, Holy Spirit, fill the hearts of the faithful and kindle in them the fire of your love.

— *when in difficulties:*
Sacred Heart of Jesus, I trust in you.

— *when you feel inclined to be cross or impatient:*
Jesus, meek and humble of heart, make my heart like yours.

— *before play:*
Lord Jesus, bless our games. Watch over us while we play.

— *in looking at a statue of the Holy Virgin:*
Hail Mary!

— *in the dark or when alone:*
Guardian Angel, keep close to me. Nothing can harm me if you are near.

— *when looking at the stars:*
Lord, the sky is full of your glory.

And you yourself will find many other times when you would like to whisper a little word to God.
'Let your hope keep you joyful, be patient in your troubles, pray at all times.' (*Rom. 12:12*)

18

PART 5 — NIGHT PRAYERS

Jesus said: 'Work while it is day, the night comes when no one can work' (*Jn 9:4*).

Another day has already passed bringing you closer to eternity. Before you go to bed never forget to say your night prayers thanking God, asking pardon and help. These prayers could help you.

O God, my Father I thank you for all the blessings and graces you have given me this day; I fear that I have not served you as well as I should have done. I now ask for light to remember where I have failed and grace to be sorry for whatever sins I have committed:
*Stop for brief examination of conscience. God is there before you; ask yourself sincerely these questions —
'Have I committed any deliberate sin today? Disobedience? Lies? Anger? etc? Am I ready to meet God?'*

My God I am sorry that I have offended you by my sins. With the help of your grace I will not sin again. I put myself trustfully into your loving hands. I ask you to keep me safe throughout the coming night, and to let my sleep renew me in strength and courage that I may serve you better tomorrow and for the rest of my life. Bless my father, my mother, my brothers and sisters, and all those for whom I ought to pray. Reward all those who have been kind to me, comfort those who are in sorrow, give strength to those in temptation.

Bring sinners to repentance, have mercy on the sick and dying. Heavenly Father, make all men find their way home to you, through Jesus Christ Our Lord and Saviour. Amen.

(If with others you could do the following:)

Concluding Prayer
Leader: May Our Lord bless and preserve you.
Response: And bring us to life everlasting.

Leader: Jesus, Mary and Joseph, I give you my heart and my soul:
Jesus, Mary and Joseph, assist me in my last agony.
Response: Jesus, Mary and Joseph, may I breathe forth my soul in peace with you.

Leader: My good angel whom God has sent to be my guardian
Response: Watch over me during the night.

Leader: May the souls of the faithful departed
Response: Through the mercy of God rest in peace. Amen.

The day is over. This morning your first thoughts were of Our Blessed Lord. Before you go to sleep, your last thoughts should be of God. This is the time to thank him for all he has done for you; to ask his forgiveness for offending him; to pray to him for others, for your family, relations, friends, the coming of Christ's kingdom, the souls in Purgatory, all those in need.

Section 2
THE BLESSED
EUCHARIST

Prayers of the Mass
'In the Mass our Redemption is renewed.'

Every Mass recalls and renews the Easter Sacrifice of Jesus, his crucifixion and his resurrection. We must join ourselves to his sacrifice by dying in him to sin, by rising with him to newness of life, by growing more and more in the grace of our Baptism, death and resurrection in Christ.

1. INTRODUCTORY RITE

Greeting
Entrance Song is sung (or said) as celebrant comes to the altar.
Celebrant: In the name of the Father and of the Son and of the Holy Spirit.

People: Amen.

The priest faces the people, extends his hands, and says the following:

C. The grace of Our Lord Jesus Christ and the love of God and the fellowship of the Holy Spirit be with you all.

P.   And also with you.

The priest may very briefly introduce the Mass of the day.

The Penitential Rite
C.   My brothers and sisters, to prepare ourselves to celebrate the sacred mysteries, let us call to mind our sins.
(*A brief pause — then all say:*)

C. & P.   I confess to almighty God and to you, my brothers and sisters, that I have sinned through my own fault in my thoughts and in my words,
in what I have done,
in what I have failed to do;
and I ask blessed Mary, ever virgin,
all the angels and saints,
and you, my brothers and sisters,
to pray for me to the Lord our God.

Absolution
C.   May almighty God have mercy on us, forgive us our sins and bring us to everlasting life.
P.   Amen.

Invocations
C.   Lord have mercy.
P.   Lord, have mercy.

C.   Christ, have mercy.
P.   Christ, have mercy.

C.   Lord, have mercy.
P.   Lord, have mercy.

The Gloria — Hymn of Praise
Glory to God in the highest,

and peace to his people on earth.
Lord God, Heavenly King,
almighty God and Father,
we worship you, we give you thanks,
we praise you for your glory.
Lord Jesus Christ, only son of the Father,
Lord God, Lamb of God,
you take away the sin of the world:
have mercy on us;
you are seated at the right hand of the Father:
receive our prayer.
You alone are the Holy One,
you alone are the Lord,
you alone the Most High,
Jesus Christ, with the Holy Spirit,
in the glory of God the Father. Amen.

Opening Prayer

*Exending hands the priest sings or says the opening
prayer.*

Let us pray... (Pause)
Amen.

2.   LITURGY OF THE WORD —
GOD SPEAKS TO US

First reading from Sacred Scripture
This is the Word of the Lord.
Thanks be to God.

Gospel

The priest bows
C.   Almighty God, cleanse my heart and my lips that I
may worthily proclaim your Gospel.

C. The Lord be with you.
P. And also with you.

C. A reading from the Holy Gospel according to...
P. Glory to you, Lord.

At the end of Gospel
C. This is the Gospel of the Lord.
P. Praise to you, Lord Jesus Christ.

Kissing the book the priest says quietly
C. May the words of the Gospel wipe away our sins.

The Homily
The priest explains the Gospel and principles of our Christian life.

The Creed — Our Profession of Faith
(Said on Sundays and Solemnities)
We believe in one God,
the Father, the Almighty
maker of heaven and earth,
of all that is seen and unseen.
We believe in one Lord, Jesus Christ,
the only Son of God,
eternally begotten of the Father,
God from God, Light from Light,
true God from true God,
begotten, not made,
one in Being with the Father.
Through him all things were made.
For us men and for our salvation he came down
　　from heaven:
by the power of the Holy Spirit
he became incarnate of the Virgin Mary, and was
　　made man.

For our sake he was crucified under Pontius Pilate;
he suffered, died, and was buried.
On the third day he rose again
according to the scriptures;
he ascended into heaven
and is seated at the right hand of the Father.
He will come again in glory to judge the living
   and the dead
and his kingdom wil have no end.
We believe in the Holy Spirit, the Lord, the giver
   of life,
who proceeds from the Father and the Son.
With the Father and the Son he is worshipped
   and glorified.
He has spoken through the prophets.
We believe in one holy, catholic and apostolic Church.
We acknowledge one baptism for the forgiveness
   of sins.
We look for the resurrection of the dead,
and the life of the world to come. Amen.

The Intercessory Prayers of the Faithful

3.   THE LITURGY OF THE EUCHARIST

The priest, standing at the altar, takes the paten with bread and, holding it slightly raised above the altar, says:

C. Blessed are you, Lord, God of all creation. Through your goodness as have this bread to offer, which earth has given and human hands have made. It will become for us the bread of life.

P. Blessed be God for ever. *(If singing is in progress, this response is omitted.)*

The priest pours wine and a little water into the chalice, saying quietly:
By the mystery of this water and wine may we come to share in the divinity of Christ, who humbled himself to share in our humanity.

Then he takes the chalice and raises it a little above the altar, saying:
C.   Blessed are you, Lord, God of all creation. Through your goodness we have this wine to offer, fruit of the vine and work of human hands. It will become our spiritual drink.
P.   Blessed be God for ever. *(If singing is in progress, this response is omitted.)*

The priest bows and says quietly:
Lord God, we ask you to receive us and be pleased with the sacrifice we offer you with humble and contrite hearts.

The priest then washes his hands at the side of the altar, saying silently:
Lord , wash away my iniquity; cleanse me from my sins.

At the centre of the altar, facing the people, the priest says:
C.   Pray, brethren, that our sacrifice may be acceptable to God, the almighty Father.
P.   May the Lord accept this sacrifice at your your hands for the praise and glory of his name, for our good, and the good of all his Church.

The priest then recites the Prayer over the gifts.

At the end of the Prayer
P.   Amen

THE EUCHARISTIC PRAYER 2

Introductory Dialogue

C. The Lord be with you.
P. And also with you.

C. Let us lift up our hearts.
P. We have lifted them up to the Lord.

C. Let us give thanks to the Lord, our God.
P. It is right to give him thanks and praise.

Preface *(We have over 100 Prefaces)*
Father, it is our duty and salvation
always and everywhere to give you thanks,
through your beloved son, Jesus Christ.
He is the word through whom you made the universe
the Saviour you sent to redeem us.
By the power of the Holy Spirit
he took flesh and was born of the Virgin Mary.
For our sake he opened his arms on the cross;
he put an end to death
and revealed the resurrection.
In this he fulfilled your will
and won for you a holy people.
And so we join the angels and the saints
in proclaiming your glory
as we sing (say):

Holy, holy, holy Lord, God of power and might,
heaven and earth are full of your glory.
    Hosanna in the highest.
Blessed is he who comes in the name of the Lord.
    Hosanna in the highest.

C.   Lord, you are holy indeed, the fountain of all
holiness.

27

Let your Spirit come upon these gifts to make them holy, so that they may become for us the Body and Blood of our Lord, Jesus Christ. Before he was given up to death, a death he freely accepted, he took bread and gave you thanks. He broke the bread, gave it to his disciples and said: **take this all of you, and eat it: this is my body which will be given up for you.**

When supper was ended, he took the cup. Again he gave you thanks and praise, gave the cup to his disciples and said: **this is the cup of my blood, the blood of the new and everlasting covenant. It will be shed for you and for all men so that sins may be forgiven. Do this in memory of me.**

C. Let us proclaim the mystery of faith:

C. and P.:   Christ has died,
Christ is risen,
Christ will come again.

or

1. Dying you destroyed our death
Rising you restored our life
Lord Jesus, come in glory.

2. When we eat this bread and drink this cup
We proclaim your death, Lord Jesus,
Until you come in glory.

3. Lord, by your cross and resurrection
You have set us free.
You are the saviour of the world.

C. In memory of his death and resurrection we offer you, Father, this life-giving bread, this saving cup. We thank you for counting us worthy to stand in your

28

presence and serve you. May all of who share in the Body and Blood of Christ be brought together in unity by the Holy Spirit.

1C. Lord, remember your Church throughout the world; make us grow in love, together with N... our Pope, N... our bishop and all the clergy.

(*In Masses for the dead the following may be said:* Remember N... whom you have called from this life. In Baptism he (she) died with Christ. May he (she) also share his resurrection.)

2C. Remember our brother and sisters who have gone to their rest in the hope of rising again; bring them and all the departed into the light of your prescence.

Have mercy on us all; make us worthy to share eternal life with Mary, the Virgin Mother of God, with the apostles and with all the saints who have done your will throughout the ages. May we praise you in union with them and give you glory through your Son, Jesus Christ.

C. Through him, with him, in him,
in the unity of the Holy Spirit,
all honour and glory is yours,
Almighty Father,
forever and ever.

All: Amen.

The Communion Rite
At the end of the Canon, the priest says to the people:
Let us pray with confidence to the Father in the words our Saviour gave us:

C. & P.: Our Father, who art in heaven, hallowed

be thy name, they kingdom come, thy will be done on earth as it is in heaven. Give us this day our daily bread and forgive us our trespasses as we forgive those who trespass against us and lead us not into temptation but deliver us from evil.

C.   Deliver us, Lord, from every evil, and grant us peace in our day. In your mercy keep us free from sin and protect us from all anxiety, as we wait in joyful hope for the coming of our saviour, Jesus Christ.

P.   For the kingdom, the power, and the glory are yours, now and forever.

C.   Lord Jesus Christ, you said to your apostles: I leave you peace, my peace I give you. Look not on our sins, but on the faith of your Church, and grant us the peace and unity of your kingdom, where you live for ever and ever.

P.   Amen.

C.   The peace of the Lord be with you always.

P.   And also with you.

Sign of Peace
Then the priest may add:
C.   Let us offer each other the sign of peace. *All make the sign of peace, (e.g. shaking hands, etc., depending on local custom) to show they are at peace with one another, before receiving Holy Communion.*

Breaking of the Bread
The priest places a small piece of the host in the chalice:
C.   May the mingling of the Body and Blood of our Lord Jesus Christ bring eternal life to us who receive it.

Meanwhile the following is sung or said:
Lamb of God, you take away the sins of the world, have mercy on us. *(twice)*
Lamb of God, you take away the sins of the world, grant us peace.

The priest joins his hands and says quietly:
Lord, Jesus Christ, son of the living God, by the will of the Father and the work of the Holy Spirit your death brought life to the world. By your Body and Blood free me from all my sins and from every evil. Keep me faithful to your teaching and never let me be parted from you.

or:

Lord Jesus Christ, with faith in your love and mercy I eat your Body and drink your Blood. Let it not bring me condemnation, but health in mind and body.

The priest genuflects, takes the host, raises it slightly above the paten and says aloud:
C. This is the Lamb of God, who takes away the sins of the world. Happy are those who are called to his supper.

He adds once: (All repeat with him)
Lord, I am not worthy to receive you, but only say the word and I shall be healed.

He receives Holy Communion saying:
C. May the Body of Christ bring me to everlasting life.
C. May the Blood of Christ bring me to everlasting life.

The people receive Holy Communion:
C. The Body of Christ.
P. Amen.   31

After Communion the priest may sit in the chair for a time. This thanksgiving time can be spent in prayerful silence or singing or repeating aloud together suitable prayers thanking God. What are you going to do? This is a suggestion only.

After Communion — *First you may close your eyes and speak to Jesus in your own words, tell him you are sorry you are not better prepared for his coming, ask his help to KNOW, LOVE, and SERVE him better each day, pray for your father, mother, brothers, sisters, friends, teachers, those in need, especially those in danger of dying in mortal sin, enemies of God. Pray for your country and all God's intentions... When you finish, you could say these: Thanksgiving Prayers after Holy Communion in next section (Never leave without a thanksgiving.)*

Concluding Rite
If there are any brief announcements, they are made now.

The priest extends his hands:
C. The Lord be with you.
P. And also with you.
V. May almighty God bless you, the Father, the Son, and the Holy Spirit.
P. Amen.

Then the priest says:
Go in the peace of Christ.

or:
The Mass is ended, go in peace.

or:

Go in peace to love and serve the Lord.

P.   Thanks be to God.

The priest then leaves the altar.

Holy Communion Scriptures
Jesus said, 'I am the living bread come down from heaven. Whoever eats this bread will live forever.'

(Jn. 6:51)

His promise: was made at Capernaum synagogue. *(See
Jn. 6:51-59.)*

His Gift: was given in Jerusalem at the Last Supper. *(See
Lk. 22:14-20.)*

His Request: 'Do this in memory of me!' *(See Lk. 22:19;
1 Cor. 11:25.)*

Our Preparation: *A holy life and true desire for loving
union with Jesus. Before receiving Holy Communion
there should be no grave sin, no eating or drinking (except
water) for one hour beforehand. The Mass itself is the best
immediate preparation.*

Thanksgiving after Holy Communion
(See Communion of Mass)

*Perhaps you might recite alone or with others the follow-
ing prayers.*

Thanksgiving prayers after Holy Communion
All repeat:

Act of Faith: O Jesus, I believe that I have received your
Sacred Body and Blood.

Act of Adoration: Jesus, my God, my Creator, I adore
you because from your hands I came and with you I am

to be happy for ever.

Act of Love: My good Jesus, I love you with all my heart; I wish to love you more every day; thank you for coming to me.

Act of Offering: O good Jesus, receive my poor offering; you have given yourself to me, now let me give myself to you.

I give you my **body** that it may be chaste and pure, I give you my **soul** that it may be free from sin, I give you my **heart** that I shall always love you. I give you every **breath** that I shall breathe and especially my last. I give you **myself** in life and in death that I may be **yours** for ever. Amen.

Pray for Yourself: O Jesus, wash away all my sins with your Precious Blood. The struggle against temptation is not yet finished. When temptation comes near me, make me strong against it. In the moment of temptation may I always say: 'Jesus mercy: Mary help!' May I lead a good life; may I die a happy death; may I receive you before I die. O Jesus, my Savior and my Redeemer, remain within my heart by your Divine Grace, never permit me to be separated from you in life or in death.

Pray for Others: O Jesus, have mercy on your holy Church, take care of it. Bless my father, my mother, my brothers and sisters; bless all I ought to pray for, as your kind heart knows how to bless them. Dear Lord Jesus, have pity on the souls in Purgatory and grant them eternal rest. Have mercy on people in danger of death today.

Soul of Christ
Soul of Christ — sanctify me,

Body of Christ — save me,
Blood of Christ — fill me,
Water from the side of Christ — purify me,
Passion of Christ — strengthen me,
O good Jesus — hear me,
Within your wounds — hide me,
Never permit me — to be separated from you,
From the evil enemy — defend me,
At the hour of my death — call me,
And command me — to come to you.
That with your angels and saints — I may praise you,
For everlasting ages. Amen.

Visits to the Blessed Sacrament
*After Mass it is customary to keep the remaining
consecrated Hosts in the tabernacle on or near the altar
in the church. Usually, a red lamp burns reminding
us of his 'Real Presence' there. The Blessed Sacrament
is a centre for public and private devotions in the
Church. Holy Communion can be brought from there
to the sick and housebound. Many popular devotions
have grown up in the Church that express our love and
gratitude to Jesus for this special type of presence, e.g.
visits to the Blessed Sacrament, Exposition, Holy
Hours, Forty Hours and Benediction. Pope John Paul
II in 1980 said, 'Public and private devotion to the
Eucharist outside Mass is also highly recommended:
for the Presence of Christ, who is adored by the faithful
in the Sacrament, derives from the Sacrifice and is
directed towards Sacramental and Spiritual
Communion.'*

Your visit to Christ in the Blessed Sacrament
Whenever you get the chance do drop into the chapel

to visit Christ Our Lord. Take Holy Water reverently. Bless yourself, walk up towards the tabernacle, genuflect (the light burning shows he is there) and kneel. Speak to him in your own way. The following may help you.

'My God, I believe you are really here present. Increase my faith. I believe in you, I hope in you, I love you above all things. You are my only real friend. I am sorry that I have served you so badly; help me to do better in the future. Sacred Heart of Jesus, may your Kingdom come everywhere!'

Speak to him about your troubles, hopes, fears, needs. Just listen! You could finish with an Act of Contrition, Morning Offering, or Spiritual Communion.

Benediction of the Most Blessed Sacrament
This ceremony is a special act of love and worship of Jesus Christ in the Eucharist.

The rite has four parts:

1. **Exposition of the Blessed Sacrament**
While the minister (priest or deacon) approaches the altar a song may be sung. From the tabernacle he takes the Sacred Host and places it on the altar in the monstrance or ciborium. This is a reminder of the essential link between the worship of the reserved Sacrament and the Eucharistic Sacrifice.

2. **Adoration**
Prayers, songs and incense are used. There should be a choice of readings, homily, prayers, periods of silence, songs or part of the Liturgy of the Hours (Divine Office), to direct the attention of the people to the worship of Christ Our Lord.

3. Benediction

Towards the end of the exposition the minister goes to the altar, genuflects and kneels. A eucharistic hymn is sung. Meanwhile the minister, while kneeling, incenses the Sacrament if it is exposed in the monstrance. Then he rises, and sings or says, **Let us Pray** *and the prayer itself. This need not be the collect for* **Corpus Christi** *but is chosen from a stock of seven prayers.*

After the prayer the priest or deacon puts on the humeral veil, genuflects, takes the monstrance or ciborium, and with it makes the sign of the cross over the people, in silence.

4. Reposition

After giving the blessing, the minister replaces the Blessed Sacrament in the tabernacle and genuflects. As he replaces it the people may sing or say an acclamation. The minister then leaves.

N.B. — *Since prayer during exposition should be addressed to Our Lord in the Blessed Sacrament, it is more fitting that prayers addressed directly to Our Lady or the saints, and devotions in their honour, be held outside the period of exposition. The recitation of the rosary draws the faithful into contemplation of Christ in his great mysteries, and would be very appropriate before exposition of the Blessed Sacrament. The litany of Loreto likewise. The 'Divine Praises' can be recited or sung here.*

Blessed be God!
Blessed be his Holy Name!
Blessed be Jesus Christ, true God and true man!
Blessed be the Name of Jesus!

Blessed be his Most Sacred Heart!

Blessed be his Most Precious Blood!

Blessed be Jesus in the Most Holy Sacrament of the Altar!

Blessed be the Holy Spirit, the Paraclete!

Blessed be the great Mother of God, Mary most Holy!

Blessed be her holy and Immaculate Conception!

Blessed be her glorious Assumption!

Blessed be the name of Mary, Virgin and Mother!

Blessed be St. Joseph, her most chaste spouse!

Blessed be God in his Angels and in his Saints!

Section 3
CONFESSION

(Sacrament of Penance and Reconciliation)

'Receive the Holy Spirit, whose sins you shall forgive
they are forgiven them' *(John 20:22-23)*

*In confession we meet Christ. Through the priest he
takes away our sins and gives us a new share in his
life and strength to live our daily life with greater hope,
confidence and love. 'Penance obtains pardon from the
mercy of God and reunites the sinner with the Church
which he has wounded by his sin' VC2. Reconciliation
with God can also be done in a public communal
penitential service, followed by private confession.*

A. Before Confession
(1) **Pray for God's help** *to make a good confession
e.g.* 'O God, help me to make a good confession.
Help me to discover my sins and the number of
times I committed them. Help me to be truly sorry
for them because they offend you, my loving
Father. Help me to resolve sincerely not to commit
these sins again. Mary, Mother of God and my
mother too help me to make this confession as if
it were my last.'

(2) **Examine your conscience** *since your last
confession and tell God you are really sorry in an
act of contrition. We must confess all mortal sins
and how many times we did them. We are not*

39

obliged to confess lesser or venial sins, but it is good to do so. The examination of conscience may be made by thinking over the commandments of God and the Church.

Our final judgment will be on love
for others. (See *Matthew 25*)

This examination of the heart may help you to prepare for confession:

Examination of the Heart
(*Based on 10 Commandments and great one of Love*)

(A) Commandments 1, 2, 3,
Have I failed in my love for God, by:

1. — Talking against my Faith or listening to such talk?
   — Neglecting prayer or praying badly?

2. — Using God's name wrongly?
   — Cursing? Bad language?
   — Being disrespectful in God's house? Avoiding it?
   — Want of respect for holy things, e.g. Sacraments?

3. — Absenting myself from Mass on the Lord's Day.
   — Coming late on Sunday? Neglecting Sabbath?

(B) Commandments 4 to 10
Have I failed in my love for others, by:

4. — Disrespect for parents, elders, authorities?

40

— Disobedience?
— Not praying for parents, relatives?
— Lack of respect for old people?
— Disobeying the laws of the state?
— (For parents) neglecting to care for wife and children?

5. — Too much smoking or drinking? Or anything harmful to my health?
— Insulting or injuring others? Despising them?
— Hatred towards others?
— Giving way to anger? Refusing to help others?
— Showing sinful ways to others? Bad example?

6. & 9. — Using sex wrongly either alone or with another?
— Desiring to use sex wrongly? Reading bad books?
— Wrong use of sex in words, dances, pictures, talk?

7. & 10. — Stealing or cheating? Bribing?
— Neglecting my work? Lazy at study?
— Not paying debts as soon as possible or restoring stolen things?
— Accepting stolen things? No restitution?
— Injuring the property of others?
— Not returning borrowed things?

8. — Lying? Especially from jealousy or hatred?

- Telling secrets or hidden sins of others? Detraction?
- Taking away the good reputation of another?
- Calumny?
- Spreading false stories or rumours that could injure another? Jealous of others?
- Not forgiving those who hurt us?
- Never praising others?

For those who go frequently to Confession (shorter form)

Missing daily prayers? Saying them carelessly? Taking God's name in vain? Cursing? Disrespect in church? Disobedience? Carelessness in my obligations to others? Anger? Small thefts? Being spiteful? Jealous? Revengeful? Omitting proper signs of love and respect? Telling lies? Being uncharitable in thought? In word? In deed?

(When you have only venial sins to confess, it is advisable to accuse yourself of sins of your past life already told in confession.)

(B) In Confession

Begin with the sign of the Cross, 'In the name of the Father and of the Son and of the Holy Spirit. Amen.'
Continue, 'Bless me, Father, for I have sinned.' It is now ... days ... weeks ... months, etc ... since my last confession. I accuse myself of the followng sins.... (*here tell your sins clearly, briefly, honestly.*) 'For these and all the sins of my past life I am heartily sorry and will try not to commit them again.'

(Now listen to the priest... He may ask a question, give

advice. He will give you a penance to say or do after confession. Before he gives you absolution or pardon you must renew your sorrow by an act of contrition like this.)

'O my God, I am heartily sorry for offending you and I hate all my sins, because I fear the loss of heaven and pains of hell, but most of all because they offend you, my God, who are so good and deserving of all my love. I firmly resolve now, with the help of your grace, never more to offend you, to avoid occasions of sin, and lead a much better life in future... Amen.'

(The priest, in the name of Christ, forgives you your sins, saying words of absolution,) 'God, the Father of mercies, through the death and resurrection of his Son has reconciled the world to himself and sent the Holy Spirit among us for forgiveness of sins; through the ministry of the Church may God give you pardon and peace, and I absolve you from your sins in the name of the Father, and of the Son, ✠ and of the Holy Spirit. Go in peace and love of Christ!'

C. After Confession

Finally, say, 'Thank you, Father!' and go joyfully apart where you can kneel or sit to say your penance. Thank God for forgiving your sins, for washing your soul clean with his precious blood. Ask him to give you his spirit of love, power and self-control. What return can I make to the Lord for all he has done for me? I can rejoice with Mary's 'Magnificat'...

N.B. — *The above is the rite of private confession. There are many other forms of penitential services and reconciliation ceremonies available. Ask your parish clergy about them.*

Section 4
THE WAY OF THE CROSS

Jesus said, 'If you wish to be my disciple
you must take up your cross daily
and follow me' (*Lk 9:23*)

*The Way of the Cross is a traditional Church devotion
by which we accompany Jesus carrying his cross from
Pilate's house to Calvary hill. There are fourteen stops
or stations on the way. At each one we stop, gaze on
Jesus with compassion, and pray. Our lives face
suffering, sickness, death as unavoidable facts of life.
What waste there? Why? We cannot explain, but gazing
on Jesus we can be sure of one thing, that he really
loves us, that he has suffered all this for our eternal
hapiness, 'because of our sins he was wounded... we
are healed by the punishment he suffered.' (Isaiah
53:51). The crosses in our daily lives, our difficulties
and sufferings, self-denials and sacrifices willingly
offered, are made sacred and profitable for salvation
by his holy cross. We share his mission.*

Making the Stations of the Cross
*It is a very good practice to visit a church and make
the Stations of the Cross. Some do this specially during
Lent and every Friday. Better still, do so daily. Think
about what you might have done at the Crucifixion.
Would you have stayed with his mother at the cross?
He died for you! There are many ways to do the*

Stations. Here is one suggested way.

Begin with Sign of Cross as usual. Say an Act of Contrition (No. 7) and Morning Prayer (No. 5). Ask Jesus to touch your heart, moving you to real compassion for him in his sufferings, sorrow for sin, amendment of life, intercession for sinners.

Before each Station:

Stand, gaze, say, 'We adore you, O Christ, and we bless you (genuflect), because by your Holy Cross you have redeemed the world.'

Look prayerfully on the picture... with love... sorrow... gratitude, then say one Hail Mary followed by 'Have mercy on us, O Lord, have mercy.'

1. Jesus is condemned to death.
2. Jesus takes up his cross.
3. Jesus falls the first time.
4. Jesus meets his sorrowing mother.
5. Jesus is helped by Simon of Cyrene.
6. Jesus' sacred face is wiped by Veronica.
7. Jesus falls the second time.
8. Jesus meets the weeping women of Jerusalem.
9. Jesus falls the third time.
10. Jesus is stripped of his garments.
11. Jesus is nailed to the cross.
12. Jesus dies on the cross.
13. Jesus is taken down from the cross.
14. Jesus is placed in the tomb.

Closing Prayers

Pray in your own words as the Spirit moves you. Finish with Prayer before a Crucifix, No. 18 and To Christ the King, No. 19.

Section 5
PRAYING TO THE SACRED HEART OF JESUS

'Persons who shall propagate this devotion shall have their names written in my Heart and they shall never be effaced.' This is one of the Twelve Promises of the Sacred Heart. It is just one other example of how much Jesus values our devotion to his Sacred Heart. This devotion is based on Scripture. The word 'heart' in the Bible occurs about 700 times, much more than the word 'God' or 'Lord'. Jesus himself used it thirty-nine times in the Gospels. When we pray to the Sacred Heart we are praying to the Person of the divine Word made flesh, Jesus Christ. ... 'Essentially this devotion is nothing else than devotion to the human and divine love of the Incarnate Word and to the love which the Heavenly Father and the Holy Spirit have for sinful men.' (Pope Pius XII). Jesus tells us, 'Learn from me for I am meek and humble in heart.' (Mt 11:29)

Apostleship of Prayer

'I put this universal Association of the Apostleship of Prayer into your hands as a precious treasure from the Pope's heart and the Heart of Christ. Put all your talents and all your strength into the accomplishment of this mission that I entrust to you today.' (*John Paul II, Rome, 13 April 1985*)

46

The Apostleship of Prayer began in 1884 as a crusade of prayer for the spreading of God's kingdom, the conversion and sanctification of sinners. The essential element is the Morning Offering. By it we offer all aspects of our lives in union with Christ's offering of himself in the Mass which continues the work of our redemption. We make our lives a prayer consecrating the world to God. The Apostleship of Prayer provides a perfect pastoral plan for holiness and apostolate.

The five point plan is:
1. The Sacrifice of the Mass and the Morning Offering.
2. Devotion to the Sacred Heart of Jesus.
3. Devotion to the Blessed Virgin Mary.
4. Loyalty to the Church and the Pope.
5. Careful attention to Prayer.

New Outlook on Life
A genuine effort to live the spirituality of the Apostleship of Prayer can transform our lives. It can give us a new outlook on the world, on people and events and fill our prayers, work, joys and sufferings with a new inner power. It can unite us most closely with Christ our Lord in the ordinary activities of every day. The love of Christ's Heart for the world and for each one of us is our inspiration. 'The Apostleship of Prayer has always distinguished itself by its commitment to spread the devotion and spirituality of the Heart of the Redeemer.' (Pope John Paul II, 1985)

Some practises of this devotion
1. Morning Offering daily.

2. Consecration of oneself personally to the Sacred Heart.
3. Consecration of your family.
4. Making reparation by prayer and self-denial.
5. Eucharistic Vigils... Holy Hours...
6. Holy Communion on First Fridays and Feast of the Sacred Heart.
7. Meditating on life of Jesus in Scriptures.
8. Making the Stations of the Cross.
9. Attending sermons, conferences about Jesus Christ.
10. Making Heroic Offering of Pioneers.
11. Promoting First Friday devotions... literature on the Sacred Heart.
12. Daily personal prayer to Sacred Heart with Blessed Virgin Mary, especially for peace and justice in family life.

Promises of the Sacred Heart

1. —I will give them all the graces necessary for their state in life.
2. —I will give peace in their families.
3. —I will console them in all their troubles.
4. —I will be their assured refuge during life, and more especially at the hour of death.
5. —I will pour abundant blessings on all their undertakings.
6. —Sinners shall find in my Heart a source and boundless ocean of mercy.
7. —Tepid souls shall become fervent.
8. —Fervent souls shall rise speedily to great perfection.

9. —I will bless the homes in which the image of my Sacred Heart shall be exposed and honoured.
10. —I will give to the priests the power to touch the most hardened hearts.
11. —Persons who shall propagate this devotion shall have their names written in my Heart and they shall never be effaced.
12. —I promise in the excess of the mercy of my Heart, that its all-powerful love will grant to all those who receive Communion on the First Friday of every month for nine consecutive months, the grace of final repentance, and that they shall not die under my displeasure, nor without receiving their Sacraments, and that my Heart shall be their secure refuge at that last hour.

Renewal of Family Act of Dedication

This renewal is made either monthly on the First Friday and/or annually on the Feast of the Most Sacred Heart of Jesus.

Lord Jesus Christ, we renew the dedication of our family to your Sacred Heart. We remember your love for us. We pledge our love in return, placing you at the centre of our hearts and of our home. We wish to live our lives in union with you and share your mission of love to all men. Lord Jesus Christ, accept this dedication and keep us always in your Sacred Heart. Amen.

Section 6
THE ROSARY
Of the Blessed Virgin Mary

'Let the entire body of the faithful pour forth persevering prayer to the Mother of God and Mother of men.... By her maternal charity, Mary cares for the brethren of her son who still journey on earth surrounded by dangers and difficulties, until they are led to their happy Fatherland' (VC2). From the first days of Christianity the faithful have multiplied ways to show their love and respect for Our Lady. Some people concentrate themselves to her in a special way with certain prayers and practices in her honour. They like to show respect to pictures, icons, statues representing her. They make pilgrimages to places like Lourdes and Fatima. They do apostolic work in organisations like the Legion of Mary, and Christian Life Communities. They recite the Litany of Loreto and especially the Rosary.

Saying the Rosary
One of the best ways to honour the Blessed Virgin Mary is to say the Rosary every day. It combines meditation on the mysteries of our faith with the recitation of vocal prayers. It honours Our Lord and his Mother, and can be said in many ways. We can think about the mysteries, or the words, or God who is present to us. A decade of the Rosary corresponds to each of the fifteen mysteries

commemorated in the Rosary. Usually five decades are recited at a time. Why not have the family Rosary each evening in your home? 'The family that prays together, stays together.'

Opening Prayers

Begin with Sign of the Cross.

Leader: O Lord, open our lips.
Response: And we shall praise your name.

Let us pray: Holy Mary, Virgin Mother of God, we come before you today to offer up this Rosary in honour of your divine son, Jesus. Help us to say it with reverence and love. Help us to share generously in the sanctifying effects of these mysteries of our salvation.

Next, you can say the Apostles' Creed as a profession of your faith, followed by one Our Father and three Hail Marys with the Glory be... in honour of the Blessed Trinity. You may just begin by announcing the Mysteries to be said. For each Mystery say one Our Father, ten Hail Marys and one Glory be...

(A) The Joyful Mysteries *(Monday and Thursday)*
1. Annunciation to Blessed Virgin Mary *(Lk. 1:28-38)*
2. Visitation to Elizabeth *(Lk. 1:38-56)*
3. Birth of Jesus *(Lk. 2:1-20)*
4. Presentation of Jesus *(Lk. 2:22-40)*
5. Finding of Jesus *(Lk. 2:41-51)*

(B) The Sorrowful Mysteries *(Tuesday and Friday)*
1. Agony in the Garden *(Lk. 22:39-55)*

2. Scourging at the Pillar   *(Mk 15:15)*
3. Crowning with Thorns   *(Mk 15:16-20)*
4. Carrying of the Cross   *(Mk 15:20-22)*
5. Crucifixion of Jesus   *(MK 15:23-29)*

(C) The Glorious Mysteries *(Sunday, Wednesday and Saturday)*

1. Resurrection of Jesus   *(Mk 16:1-18)*
2. Ascension   *(Lk 24:44-53)*
3. Descent of Holy Spirit   *(Acts 2:1-47)*
4. Assumption of the Blessed Virgin Mary   *(Sir 24:9-10)*
5. Crowning as Queen of Heaven   *(Rev 12:1)*

Closing Prayers
Hail Holy Queen... see No. 9 in Most Useful Prayers above.

Let us Pray: O God, whose only-begotten Son, by his life, death and resurrection, has purchased for us the rewards of eternal life; grant, we beseech you, that meditating on these Mysteries, in the most holy Rosary of the Blessed Virgin Mary, we may both imitate what they contain, and obtain what they promise, through the same Christ Our Lord.
Response: Amen.

Leader: May the divine assistance remain always with us.
Response: May the souls of the faithful departed through the mercy of God, rest in peace. Amen.

Thy Kingdom Come!

Live, Jesus, live! so live in me
That all I do be done by thee!
And grant that all I think and say, and read and write,
May be thy thoughts and words this day,
   and all tonight;
Each beat of heart and breath of mine
May be, Sweet Jesus, always thine!

Litany of Loreto

Lord, have mercy	Lord, have mercy
Christ, have mercy	Christ, have mercy
Lord, have mercy	Lord, have mercy
God the Father in heaven	have mercy on us
God the Son, Redeemer of the world	have mercy on us
God the Holy Spirit	have mercy on us
Holy Trinity, one God	have mercy on us
Holy Mary	pray for us
Holy Mother of God	pray for us
Holy virgin of virgins	pray for us
Mother of Christ	pray for us
Mother of the Church	pray for us
Mother of divine grace	pray for us
Mother most pure	pray for us
Mother of chaste love	pray for us
Mother and virgin	pray for us
Sinless mother	pray for us
Dearest of mothers	pray for us
Model of motherhood	pray for us

Mother of good counsel	pray for us
Mother of our Creator	pray for us
Mother of our Saviour	pray for us
Virgin most wise	pray for us
Virgin rightly praised	pray for us
Virgin rightly renowned	pray for us
Virgin most powerful	pray for us
Virgin gentle in mercy	pray for us
Faithful virgin	pray for us
Mirror of justice	pray for us
Throne of wisdom	pray for us
Cause of our joy	pray for us
Shrine of the Spirit	pray for us
Glory of Israel	pray for us
Vessel of selfless devotion	pray for us
Mystical Rose	pray for us
Tower of David	pray for us
Tower of ivory	pray for us
House of gold	pray for us
Ark of the covenant	pray for us
Gate of heaven	pray for us
Morning Star	pray for us
Health of the sick	pray for us
Refuge of sinners	pray for us
Comfort of the troubled	pray for us
Help of Christians	pray for us
Queen of angels	pray for us
Queen of patriarchs and prophets	pray for us
Queen of apostles and martyrs	pray for us

Queen of confessors and virgins	pray for us
Queen of all saints	pray for us
Queen conceived without original sin	pray for us
Queen assumed into heaven	pray for us
Queen of the Rosary	pray for us
Queen of peace	pray for us
Lamb of God, you take away the sins of the world	have mercy on us
Lamb of God, you take away the sins of the world	have mercy on us
Lamb of God, you take away the sins of the world	have mercy on us

The minister then says:
Pray for us, holy Mother of God.

And all respond:
That we may become worthy of the promises of Christ.

The minister invites the people to pray:
Let us pray.

After a brief pause for silent prayer, the minister continues:
Eternal God,
let your people enjoy constant health in mind and body.
Through the intercession of the Virgin Mary free us
from the sorrows of this life and lead us to happiness
in the life to come.

Grant this through Christ our Lord.

All respond:
Amen.

Litany of the Blessed Virgin Mary

Lord, have mercy	Lord, have mercy
Christ, have mercy	Christ, have mercy
Lord, have mercy	Lord, have mercy
God the Father in heaven	have mercy on us
God the Son, Redeemer of the world	have mercy on us
God the Holy Spirit	have mercy on us
Holy Trinity, one God	have mercy on us
Holy Mary	pray for us
Holy Mother of God	pray for us
Most honoured of virgins	pray for us
Chosen daughter of the Father	pray for us
Mother of Christ the King	pray for us
Glory of the Holy Spirit	pray for us
Virgin daughter of Zion	pray for us
Virgin poor and humble	pray for us
Virgin gentle and obedient	pray for us
Handmaid of the Lord	pray for us
Mother of the Lord	pray for us
Helper of the Redeemer	pray for us
Full of grace	pray for us
Fountain of beauty	pray for us
Model of virtue	pray for us

Finest fruit of the redemption	pray for us
Perfect disciple of Christ	pray for us
Untarnished image of the Church	pray for us
Woman transformed	pray for us
Woman clothed with the sun	pray for us
Woman crowned with stars	pray for us
Gentle Lady	pray for us
Gracious Lady	pray for us
Our Lady	pray for us
Joy of Israel	pray for us
Splendour of the Church	pray for us
Pride of the human race	pray for us
Advocate of peace	pray for us
Minister of holiness	pray for us
Champion of God's people	pray for us
Queen of love	pray for us
Queen of mercy	pray for us
Queen of peace	pray for us
Queen of angels	pray for us
Queen of patriarchs and prophets	pray for us
Queen of apostles and martyrs	pray for us
Queen of confessors and virgins	pray for us
Queen of all saints	pray for us
Queen conceived without original sin	pray for us

Queen assumed into heaven	pray for us
Queen of all earth	pray for us
Queen of heaven	pray for us
Queen of the universe	pray for us
Lamb of God, you take away the sins of the world	spare us, O Lord
Lamb of God, you take away the sins of the world	hear us, O Lord
Lamb of God, you take away the sins of the world	have mercy on us

Minister:
Pray for us, O glorious Mother of the Lord.

All respond:
That we may become worthy of the promises of Christ.

The minister concludes the litany with the following prayer:
God of mercy,
listen to the prayers of your servants who have honoured your handmaid Mary as mother and queen. Grant that by your grace we may serve you and our neighbour on earth and be welcomed into your eternal kingdom.

We ask this through Christ our Lord.

All respond:
Amen.

Prayers to the Blessed Virgin Mary

The following prayers are suitable for private prayer.
They may also be adapted for use in one of the services
contained in this book.

Canticle of Mary

The 'Canticle of Mary' or 'Magnificat' is sung in the
celebration of Evening Prayer each day. The text is
taken from the Gospel according to Luke 2:29-32.

My soul proclaims the greatness of the Lord,
my spirit rejoices in God my Saviour
for he has looked with favour on his lowly servant.

From this day all generations will call me blessed:
the Almighty has done great things for me,
and holy is his Name.

He has mercy on those who fear him
in every generation.

He has shown the strength of his arm,
he has scattered the proud in their conceit.

He has cast down the mighty from their thrones,
and has lifted up the lowly.

He has filled the hungry with good things,
and the rich he has sent away empty.

He has filled the hungry with good things,
and the rich he has sent away empty.

He has come to the help of his servant Israel
for he remembered his promise of mercy,
the promise he made to our fathers,
to Abraham and his children for ever.

Regina Caeli

The 'Regina Caeli' is a twelfth century antiphon for Evening Prayer during the Easter Season. Since the thirteenth century, it has been used as the seasonal antiphon in honour of the Blessed Virgin after Night Prayer. From 1743, it has replaced the Angelus in the Easter Season.

Queen of heaven, rejoice, alleluia.
The Son whom you merited to bear, alleluia,
has risen as he said, alleluia.
Pray to God for us, alleluia.

V.   Rejoice and be glad, O Virgin Mary, alleluia.
R.   For the Lord has truly risen, alleluia.

Let us pray.

God of life,
you have given joy to the world by the resurrection
of your Son, our Lord Jesus Christ.
Through the prayers of his mother, the Virgin Mary,
bring us to the happiness of eternal life.

We ask this through Christ our Lord.

R.   Amen.

Sub Tuum Praesidium, Ancient Prayer to the Virgin

This prayer, known in Latin as 'Sub tuum praesidium' and first found in a Greek papyrus, c. 300, is the oldest known prayer to the Virgin.

We turn to you for protection,
holy Mother of God.
Listen to our prayers
and help us in our needs.

Save us from every danger,
glorious and blessed Virgin.

Mary, Help of Those in Need

'Mary, Help of Those in Need' was formerly the Magnificat antiphon from the Common of the Blessed Virgin Mary, Evening Prayer.

Holy Mary,
help those in need,
give strength to the weak,
comfort the sorrowful,
pray for God's people,
assist the clergy,
intercede for religious.

May all who seek your help
experience your unfailing protection.
Amen.

Our Lady of Guadalupe

In the dioceses of the United States of America, Our Lady of Guadalupe is celebrated on December 12. The following is the Opening Prayer of the memorial of Our Lady of Guadalupe.

God of power and mercy,
you blessed the Americas at Tepeyac
with the presence of the Virgin Mary of Gudulupe.
May her prayers help all men and women
to accept each other as brothers and sisters.

Through your justice present in our hearts
may your peace reign in the world.

We ask this through our Lord Jesus Christ, your Son,
who lives and reigns with you and the Holy Spirit,
one God, for ever and ever.
Amen.

A Child's Prayer to Mary

*This prayer is from the hymn 'Memento rerum
conditor.' It is also found as the last verse in some
versions of the hymn 'Quem terra pontus aethera.'*

Mary, mother whom we bless,
full of grace and tenderness,
defend me from the devil's power
and greet me in my dying hour.

A Prayer for Vocations

*This prayer was prepared by the Secretariat of the
Bishops' Committee on Vocations, National
Conference of Catholic Bishops, in 1987.*

Hail Mary, full of grace;
all generations call you blessed.

Hail Mother of God; when asked by the angel
  to bear the Son of the Most High,
  filled with faith, you responded:
  'Let it be done unto me.'

Holy Mother of Jesus, at the wedding feast at Cana,
  you prompted your Son to perform his first sign.

  Be with us as we discern our life's work
  and guide us in the way we are called to follow
  in the footsteps of your Son.

Holy Mother of the Saviour, at the foot of the cross

you mourned the death of your only Son.

Bless and embrace the loving parents of all priests,
deacons, brothers, and sisters.

Holy Mother of the Good Shepherd,
turn your motherly care to this nation.

Intercede for us to the Lord of the harvest
to send more labourers to the harvest
in this land dedicated to your honour.

Queen of Peace, Mirror of Justice, Health of the Sick,
inspire vocations in our time.

Let the word of your Son be made flesh anew
in the lives of persons anxious to proclaim
the good news of everlasting life.

Amen.

A Prayer to Mary from the Act of Entrusting the World to Mary by Pope John Paul II

Hail to you, Mary,
who are wholly united to the redeeming consecration
of your Son!

Mother of the Church,
enlighten the people of God along the paths of faith,
hope and love.
Help us to live in the truth of the consecration of Christ
for the entire human family of the modern world.

In entrusting to you, O Mother,
the world, all individuals and peoples, we also entrust
to you this very consecration of the world, placing it
in your motherly heart.

Immaculate Heart of Mary,
help us to conquer the menace of evil, which so easily
takes root in the hearts of the people of today, and
whose immeasurable effects already weigh down upon
our modern world and seem to block the paths toward
the future.

From famine and war, deliver us.
From nuclear war, from incalculable self-destruction,
from every kind of war, deliver us.
From sins against human life from its very beginning,
deliver us.
From hatred and from the demeaning of the dignity
of the children of God, deliver us.
From every kind of injustice in the life of society, both
national and international, deliver us.
From readiness to trample on the commandments of
God, deliver us.
From attempts to stifle in human hearts the very truth
of God, deliver us.
From the loss of awareness of good and evil, deliver
us.
From sins against the Holy Spirit, deliver us.

Accept, O Mother of Christ,
this cry laden with the sufferings of all individual
human beings, laden with the sufferings of whole
societies.

Help us with the power of the Holy Spirit to conquer
all sin: individual sin and the 'sin of the world', sin
in all its manifestations.
Let there be revealed once more in the history of the
world the infinite saving power of the redemption: the

power of merciful love.
May it put a stop to evil.
May it transform consciences.
May your immaculate heart reveal for all the light of
hope.

Amen.

Prayer to Saint Joseph

*While the Fathers of the Church praised Saint Joseph
in their writings, devotion to the husband of Mary arose
in the Western Church only in the fifteenth century.
Pope Leo XIII (1810-1903) encouraged the recitation
of this prayer after the Rosary and the Litany of Loreto
during the month of October.*

Blessed Joseph, husband of Mary, be with us this day.

You protected and cherished the Virgin;
loving the Child Jesus as your Son,
you rescued him from danger of death.
Defend the Church; the household of God,
purchased by the blood of Christ.

Guardian of the holy family,
be with us in our trials.
May your prayers obtain for us
the strength to flee from error
and wrestle with the powers of corruption
so that in life we may grow in holiness
and in death rejoice in the crown of victory.

Amen.

Litany of Saint Joseph

The following Litany of Saint Joseph was approved for

devotional use by Pope Saint Pius X (1835-1914).

Lord, have mercy,	Lord, have mercy
Christ, have mercy	Christ, have mercy
Lord, have mercy	Lord, have mercy
God our Father in heaven	have mercy on us
God the Son, Redeemer of the world	have mercy on us
God the Holy Spirit	have mercy on us
Holy Trinity, one God	have mercy on us
Holy Mary	pray for us
Saint Joseph	pray for us
Noble son of the House of David	pray for us
Light of patriarchs	pray for us
Husband of the Mother of God	pray for us
Guardian of the Virgin	pray for us
Foster father of the Son of God	pray for us
Faithful guardian of Christ	pray for us
Head of the holy family	pray for us
Joseph, chaste and just	pray for us
Joseph, prudent and brave	pray for us
Joseph, obedient and loyal	pray for us
Pattern of patience	pray for us
Lover of poverty	pray for us
Model of workers	pray for us
Example of parents	pray for us
Guardian of virgins	pray for us
Pillar of family life	pray for us

Comfort of the troubled	pray for us
Hope of the sick	pray for us
Patron of the dying	pray for us
Terror of evil spirits	pray for us
Protector of the Church	pray for us

Lamb of God, you take away the sins of the world	have mercy on us
Lamb of God, you take away the sins of the world	have mercy on us
Lamb of God, you take away the sins of the world	have mercy on us

V. God made him master of his household.

R. And put him in charge of all that he owned.

Let us pray.

Almighty God,
in your infinite wisdom and love you chose Joseph to
be the husband of Mary, the mother of your Son.
As we enjoy his protection on earth may we have the
help of his prayers in heaven.

We ask this through Christ our Lord.

Amen.

Section 7
PRAYING
WITH THE BIBLE

'Ever since you were a child you have known the Holy Scriptures which are able to give you the wisdom that leads to salvation through faith in Christ Jesus.' *(2 Tim. 3:15)*

'Prayer should accompany the reading of scripture so that God and man may talk together.' *(VC2)*

See also: 2 Pt. 1:2; Jn. 20:31; Pss. 119, 18, 11; Acts 2:42-47; Jas. 1:22; Jer. 15:16; 1 Sam. 3:10.

1.   God speaks to us first
He speaks to us continually. He reveals himself to us in many ways: Through Jesus Christ, his Word, through the Church, through visible creation, through events of our lives, through Holy Scripture. How can we meet him in the Bible?

2.   God invites us to listen
Our response to God speaking to us must be to listen to what he is saying to us. This is the basic attitude of prayer.

3. How to listen — Silence, Solitude, Scripture

Silence and **solitude** *are a great help to concentrate fully on God and his message to you. Select a passage from Scripture, five to ten verses. Relax, focus on God as present with you now, ask his grace to be open to his Spirit speaking to you, to listen to what he says.*

Scripture — *begin reading slowly and attentively. Read the complete passage once. Re-read it more slowly, pausing whenever some words or phrases strike you, carry a special meaning or message for you. Listen... pause... 'What are you telling me here, Lord?... What do you want me to do?...' ... 'Speak, Lord, your servant is listening.' (1 Sam 3:9) Remember, God will speak to you in his own way. Don't be in a hurry to move on. Speak to him about your hopes, fears, problems, joys, sorrows. Finish with short prayers like the Morning Offering.*

Summary: *Choose a passage from Scripture. Adopt a place where you have silence, solitude. Posture, relaxed, peaceful. The presence of God is the secret of prayer... Be aware... respond. Pray the passage... reading... listening...*

4. Group Bible Prayer

'Where two or three come together in my name...' (Mt 18:20.) There is a special value in praying with other Christians. Lumko Missionary Institute were told to find a way to make the Bible understandable and useable for everyone. They invented the famous 'Seven Steps' of Bible meditation for group use. Here they are in brief:

69

(1) **We invite the Lord** to open us to the living presence of the Risen Christ.

(2) **We read the text.** The facilitator announces the text, invites a volunteer to read it.

(3) **We look at the text again.** No preaching or discussion! What important words and verses do we find? We read the text again.

(4) **We let God speak to us.** Silence for two to five minutes.

(5) **We share** what we have heard in our hearts. No preaching or discussing.

(6) **We search together.** What does the Lord want us to do? Which word will we take home?

(7) **We pray together.** The facilitator invites everyone to pray as the Spirit moves...

Conclusion:

'We needed a method by which everyone and anyone could simply sit down in Jesus' presence, to spend time there and be touched by him! And we discovered that the easiest way for average Christians to gain access to sacred Scripture was through meditation.' *(Fr. Hirmer)*

Some inspired prayers (Psalms)

Psalm 103: How good God is to mankind.

104: How great God is.

105: How faithful God is to mankind.

136: Our gratitude to God.

139: How close God is to me.

106: How often we reject god.

38: I cry to God in my need.

51: I ask God for mercy.

Section 8
THE CHURCH'S YEAR

The Church celebrates the memory of Christ's saving work on appointed days in the course of the year. Each day is made holy through the liturgical celebrations of God's people, especially the eucharistic sacrifice and the divine office. By means of devotional exercises, instruction, prayer and works of penance and mercy, the Church completes the formation of the faithful during the various seasons of the liturgical year.

Sunday
The Church celebrates the Paschal Mystery, the memorial of the Death and Resurrection of Christ, on the first day of the week, known as the Lord's Day or Sunday. Sunday should be considered the original feast day. The observance of Sunday begins with the evening before.

The Easter Triduum
The Easter Triduum of the passion, death and resurrection of Christ is the highest point of the entire liturgical year. The Great Three Days begin with the evening Mass of the Lord's Supper on Holy Thursday, reach a high point in the Easter Vigil, and close with evening prayer on Easter Sunday. On Good Friday,

and if possible, also on Holy Saturday, the Easter Fast is observed everywhere. The Easter Vigil, on the night when Christ arose from the dead, is considered the 'mother of all vigils': during it the Church keeps watch, awaiting the resurrection of Christ and celebrating the sacraments especially of Baptism and Eucharist.

Easter Season
The fifty days from Easter to Pentecost are celebrated as one feastday, sometimes called the 'great Sunday'. The Ascension is usually celebrated on the fortieth day after Easter. The days between Ascension and Pentecost celebrate a novena of prayer for the coming of the Holy Spirit.

Season of Lent
The season of Lent is a preparation for the celebration of Easter. The liturgy prepares the catechumens, who are preparing to be baptised, for the celebration of the Paschal mystery, through the several stages of Christian initiation: it also prepares the faithful, who recall their baptism and do penance. Lent lasts from Ash Wednesday to the Mass of the Lord's Supper. Ashes are distributed on Ash Wednesday which is also a day of universal fasting. The Sixth Sunday of Lent marks the beginning of Holy Week and is called Passion Sunday or Palm Sunday.

Christmas Season
The Christmas season celebrates the birth of our Lord and his early manifestations. It runs from First Vespers of Christmas until the Sunday after Epiphany.

Christmas has its own octave arranged as follows: Sunday within the octave — feast of the Holy Family: 26 December — feast of St Stephen: 27 December — feast of St John, apostle: 28 December — feast of Holy Innocents: 29, 30, 31 December — are days within the octave: 1 January — solemnity of Mary, Mother of God. Epiphany is usually celebrated on 6 January. The season closes on the Sunday after 6 January — the feast of the Baptism of the Lord.

Advent
The season of Advent has a twofold character. It is a season when minds are directed to Christ's second coming at the end of time; and from 17 December a time of preparation for Christmas when the first coming of God's Son to us is recalled. Advent begins on the Sunday nearest 30 November, and has four Sundays.

Ordinary Time
On the other Sundays of the year the mystery of Christ in all its fullness is celebrated, and these Sundays are known as Sundays in Ordinary Time.

Other Solemnities
Trinity Sunday celebrates the mystery of Father, Son and Holy Spirit on the Sunday after Pentecost.
Corpus Christi or **The Body and Blood of Christ** is celebrated on the Thursday after Trinity Sunday.
The Sacred Heart of Jesus on the Friday after the Second Sunday after Pentecost.
Christ the King is celebrated on the last Sunday of Ordinary Time.

Section 9
SOME FEAST DAYS

Jan   1   Mary, the Mother of God
         25   Conversion of St Paul

Feb   2   Presentation of Jesus in the Temple
         22   St Peter, First Pope

Mar   8   John of God
         17   Patrick
         19   Joseph, the husband of Mary
         25   Annunciation by the Angel Gabriel to Mary

Apr   25   Mark, Evangelist

May   1   Joseph, the Worker
          3   Philip and James, Apostles
         14   Matthias, Apostle
         31   Visitation by Mary to Elizabeth

June   3   Uganda Martyrs, Charles Lwanga and Companions
         11   Barnabas, Apostle
         24   Birth of John the Baptist
         29   Peter and Paul, Apostles

July   3   Thomas, Apostle
         25   James, Apostle
         31   Ignatius Loyola

Aug	8	Dominic
	15	Assumption of Mary to Heaven
	22	Queenship of Mary
	24	Bartholomew, Apostle
	29	Beheading of John the Baptist

Sept	8	Birthday of Mary
	15	Our Lady of Sorrows
	21	Matthew, Apostle and Evangelist
	27	Vincent de Paul
	29	Archangels Michael, Gabriel and Raphael

Oct	1	Teresa of the Child Jesus
	4	Francis of Assisi
	7	Our Lady of the Rosary
	18	Luke, Evangelist
	28	Simon and Jude, Apostles

Nov	1	All Saints
	2	Remembrance of the dead
	21	Presentation of Mary in the Temple
	30	Andrew, Apostle

Dec	3	Francis Xavier
	8	Immaculate Conception of the Virgin Mary
	21	Peter Canisius
	25	Christmas, the birth of Jesus
	27	John, Apostle and Evangelist

Section 10
A SUMMARY OF
CHRISTIAN DOCTRINE

Christ is our Teacher, 'You call me teacher and lord, and you are right, for so I am.' (*John 13:13*) The Christian way of life is the way of Christ. He is himself the Way, the Truth and the Life. (*John 14:5*) He revealed to us the Father, and he taught us by words and by example how to live our earthly lives. He draws us to holiness. He is the centre of God's entire plan of salvation.

1. What is the centre of the Christian Faith?
The central element is composed of Faith in God, in Jesus of Nazareth as the decisive Sacrament of God, in the Church as the Sacrament of Christ, and in the Sacraments, particularly Baptism and Eucharist. Faith is necessary for salvation. Jesus said, 'Whoever believes and is baptised will be saved; whoever does not believe will be condemned.' (*Mark 16:16*)

2. Where can I find a good summary of the Christian Faith?
The Apostles' Creed contains an approved summary of our Christian beliefs. Already in the second century in the Christian Church in Rome, candidates for

Baptism were asked three questions as a summary of the faith. These were: 1) Do you believe in God, the almighty Father, maker of heaven and earth? 2) Do you believe in Jesus Christ, his only Son, our Lord, who was conceived by the Holy Spirit of the Virgin Mary, who suffered, was crucified, and died, and rose again, and will come to judge the living and the dead? 3) Do you believe in the Holy Spirit, in the Holy Catholic Church, the Communion of Saints, the forgiveness of sins, the resurrection of the body and life everlasting?

These three questions are the basis for the Apostles' Creed and also for the other great creeds of the ancient Church: the Nicene Creed (325 AD) and the Athanasian Creed (about 400 AD). The triple form is already an indication of the Christian faith in the threefold reality of God as he has revealed himself in Christ. Almost all Christians today accept these professions of faith made by the undivided Church in great Councils in the first four centuries of Christianity.

3. Can you give me the words of the Apostles' Creed?
You can find them in this prayerbook in section 1, N. 8. Apostles' Creed (our profession of faith). Most catechisms explain the Creed in great detail.

Basic Beliefs in Apostles' Creed
1. *Christian Faith:* I believe in, trust in, commit myself wholly to God.
2. *God:* He is Creator infinite, Father, Holy Trinity.
3. *Jesus Christ:* Son of God, Saviour, Teacher, Healer, Judge, Reward.

4. *Holy Spirit:* Third Person of Trinity, Sanctifer, Unifer, Guide.
5. *Holy Catholic Church:* Sacrament of Salvation, Body of Christ, People of God.
6. *Communion of Saints:* Church family on earth, in Purgatory, in Heaven.
7. *Forgiveness of sins:* Reconciliation through Baptism, Penance, Contrition.
8. *Resurrection of Body:* With glorified body like Risen Jesus.
9. *Life Everlasting:* Our lasting reward, perfect eternal happiness with God and the saved.

4. Please summarise briefly the doctrine in the Apostles' Creed.

(A) God
(Gen. 1:1-17; Wis. 13:1-19; Acts 17:26-27; Heb. 1:1-14; Jn. 1:1-18; Rom. 1:19-20; Heb. 4:13; Pss. 10, 104, 139)

There is only one God, our first beginning and last end. He is our Creator by our birth, our Father by baptism, our Judge at death. He is the Father of our Lord Jesus Christ. In God there are three Persons really distinct and equal in all things, the Father, the Son and the Holy Spirit. This is called the mystery of the Blessed Trinity. 'God loved the world so much that he gave his only Son, so that everyone who believes in him may not die but may have eternal life.' *(Jn. 3:16)*

(B) Our Savior Jesus Christ
(Mt.1:1-25; Lk.1:26-38, 2:1-14; Phil.1:5-11; Acts

2:32-36; 1 Tim 1:15; Acts 10:34-43; Mt 11:1-5; Lk 4:16-22, 6:25-34, 15:1-32, 6:12-14. Story of Jesus in the Four Gospels.)

God the Son became man (the Incarnation) like us. His mother is Mary who conceived him by the Holy Spirit. He was born at Bethlehem about 2,000 years ago. Jesus brought us from his Father the Good News (Gospel) of Salvation, and by his death opened up to us the way to Heaven. He rose from the dead and lives on in his Church by the power and guidance of his Holy Spirit, the Gift of the Father. 'The Virgin Mary is acknowledged and honoured as being truly the Mother of God and Mother of the Redeemer.' (*VC2*). On the last Day Jesus will come in glory to judge everyone on the law of love. (*Mt 25:31-46*)

(C)   Christ's Church
(Mt 16:18-19; Tit 2:14; Eph 5:25-26; Acts 1:15, 2:14; Mt 28:18-20; Jn 21:15-17; Rom 12:4-5. VC on Church).

Christ founded a Church to carry on his saving work till the end of time. The Church is the continuation of Christ in the world and the sacrament of his presence. The Catholic believes what the Church teaches because he recognises Christ's authority in the Church. He tries to help the work of the Church because he sees it as the work of Christ (*Mt 28:20*). In a real way the Church is Christ, made one with him as his Mystical Body. *(Jn 15:15; 1 Cor 12:27:13, 10:16-17; Col 1:18.)* The Second Vatican Council spoke specially of the Church as the People of God. The Church is made up of all the members of the family of faith. Pope, laymen, bishops, religious, priests, and members of every degree and vocation, all gathered together in Christ, are the Church. We are Christ's people, the People of God. All receive the same Spirit in Baptism, all are nourished with the one Eucharist, all share the same hope of everlasting life. All are children of God.

The true Church has certain qualities by which it can be identified. In many ancient creeds the Church is described as 'one, holy, catholic, and apostolic'. These are qualities to be looked for not only in the universal Church, but in the local churches, parishes and even in the individual Christian. Because the Church is brought together and filled with the one Spirit of Jesus, there can be only **one Church**. The prayer of all Christians, divided through human frailty and the events of history, must be for the Spirit to lead all towards the unity that Christ desires. The Holy Spirit is the Sanctifier and fills the Church so we can speak of a **holy Church**. The witness of countless saints throughout the history, the quiet workings of holiness at all times among Christians bring us to acknowledge the sanctifying power at work even among what is still a 'church of sinners'. Christ came to bring salvation to all; it is a **Catholic Church** because it is open to all who are ready to accept the Gospel and be baptised. The Church is built on the foundation of the apostles: it is an **apostolic Church** since it is faithful to the mission of the apostles and rooted in their belief.

Church membership
The Catholic Church steadfastly believes that it is the

one and only Church of Jesus Christ. To say this is certainly not to say that other Christian communities are without value, or insincere, or that their members are not deeply devoted to Christ. In the words of Second Vatican Council: 'This is the unique Church of Christ which in the creed we avow as one, holy, catholic and apostolic. After his resurrection our Saviour handed her over to Peter to be shepherded *(cf. Jn. 21:17)*. He committed her to him and to the other apostles that they might propagate and rule her *(cf. Mt. 28:18ff)*. Her he erected for all ages as 'the pillar and bulwark of the truth' *(1 Tim. 3:15)*. This Church, constituted and organised in this world as a society, subsists in the Catholic Church, governed by the successor of Peter and the Bishops in communion with him' *(L.G.8)*. To say that Christ's Church 'subsists' in the Catholic Church is to say that Christ's Church is a concrete historical reality, and that that concrete reality is found in the living, visible Catholic Church.

From its earliest days the Church has proclaimed that Christ is the only Saviour, and that people lay hold to eternal life only by coming to him. 'Outside the Church there is no salvation,' St Cyprian taught in the third century. The Church has always taught this doctrine. But this is no fierce proclamation that those who, through no fault of their own, have not come to recognize Christ's presence in the Church and his command to come to this life will be excluded from salvation. Certainly those who earnestly intend in their hearts to do all that God requires of them are not excluded from the hope of eternal life, as they are excluded from a certain membership by desire in the

Church. Many who are not members in the full sense of the Catholic Church are surely Christ's own, and linked to the saving sacrament of his Church by many bonds. 'The Catholic Church accepts them with respect and affection as brothers and sisters. For these who believe in Christ and have been properly baptised are brought into a certain, though imperfect, communion with the Catholic Church.' (*L. G. 8*)

But the Catholic Church is not an organisation which is merely optional. For this reason, those who, aware of the fact that the Catholic Church was made necessary by God through Jesus Christ, would yet refuse to enter her or persevere in her, could not be saved.' (*L. G. 14*) This is a matter of faithfulness to Jesus Christ. It is he who invites all to life, and there 'is no other name under heaven given among men by which we must be saved.' (*Acts 4:12*)

Section 11
HOW DO I LIVE MY FAITH?

'Not everyone who calls me, "Lord! Lord!" will enter the kingdom of Heaven, but only those who do what my Father in Heaven wants them to do.' (*Mt 7:21*) St James (*2:14-26*) warns us strongly about this, 'My brothers, what good is it for someone to say that he has faith if his actions do not prove it? ... if faith is alone and includes no actions it is dead.' When the rich young man asked Jesus, 'Good teacher, what must I do to receive eternal life?' he was told to keep the commandments. (*Lk 18:18-21*). For perfect holiness he was told to give away his wealth, 'then come and follow Me!'

1. How can I follow Jesus and do what pleases him?
He tells me, 'If you love me you will keep my commandments.' (*John 14:15*). Elsewhere John says, 'If someone says he knows God, but does not obey his commands, such a person is a liar' (*1 John 2:4*).

2. Which commandment is the greatest of all?
One day a scribe asked Jesus this question. Jesus told him, 'You must love the Lord your God with all your heart, with all your soul, with all your mind and with

all your strength. The second is this: you must love your neighbour as yourself. There is no commandment greater than these.' *(Mk. 12:28-31; cf. Deut. 6:5)*

3. What about the commandments that God gave us through Moses?

These are ten signposts for all on the way to Heaven. The first three deal with our duty to God; the others with our duty to our neighbour. *(Ex. 20:1-17; Mt. 5:17-48)*

1. I am the Lord your God. You shall not have other gods besides me.
2. You shall not take the name of the Lord, your God, in vain.
3. Remember to keep holy the Sabbath day.
4. Honour your father and your mother.
5. You shall not kill.
6. You shall not commit adultery.
7. You shall not steal.
8. You shall not bear false witness against your neighbour.
9. You shall not covet your neighbour's wife.
10. You shall not covet you neighbour's goods.

4. What is God teaching us in these commandments?

(a) The loving service of God comes before everything else.
(b) To serve him properly we must have unconditional respect in thought, word, deed for our neighbour who is every other human being on the face of the earth.
(c) Certain types of acts conflict with love of God and respect for our neighbour.

5. How are we to pray?

Jesus is the model and teacher of prayer. The Gospels often describe Jesus at prayer *(Lk. 3; 21:5; 16:9; 29:10; 21:11; 1:22, 32)*. He prayed, publicly as well as privately, before the most important acts and decisions of his ministry *(Lk. 4:1; Mt. 14:23; Heb. 5:7)*. Jesus directed his whole life according to his Father's will and was in continuous contact with him *(Jn. 1:51, 4; 34:8; 29:11, 41)*. Jesus by his example and command asks us to pray always. How to pray at all times has been the question Christians have always asked. Some groups at times in history have set out to live lives of prayer alone, and these contemplative communities have had to modify their lives according to circumstances. The ordinary Christian usually recognises fixed times for prayer that sanctify the rest of his or her daily living. The Church's Offices of Morning Prayer and Evening Prayer are being celebrated by more and more people as the Church has requested. Many people give time to mental prayer or meditation, and there are many other forms of prayer. The rule has been expressed that one should pray in the way one can, not in the way one can't!

6. How do we find Christ in the Liturgy and Sacraments?

Christ is always present in his Church, especially in her liturgical celebrations. There is present in the sacrifice of the Mass, not only in the person of his minister... but especially under the Eucharistic species. By his power he is present in the Sacraments, so that when a man baptises it is really Christ who baptises. He is present in his Word since it is he himself who speaks when the holy Scriptures are read in the Church. He is present when the church prays or sings, for he promised, 'Where two or three' ... *(Mt. 18-20)*. From this it follows that every liturgical celebration, because it is an action of Christ, the priest, and his Body the Church, is a sacred action surpassing all others. *(VC2 Const. Lit. 7.)*

7. How do the Sacraments increase our Christ-life?

'I have come that you may have life — life in all its fullness' *(Jn. 18:10)*. Christ gave us the seven Sacraments as sacred signs signifying and causing his divine life in us. They are Baptism, Confirmation, Eucharist, Penance, Anointing of Sick, Holy Orders, Matrimony. They correspond to the different stages of our life experience and what we need on our way to Heaven. It is Christ himself who acts through the minister of the sacrament.

1st **Baptism:** By this sacrament Christ frees us from all sin, makes us children of God his Father, his own brothers and sisters, members of his Church with the promise of eternal life in Heaven *(Mt. 28:18-20; Mk. 16:16; Acts 2:38; Jn. 3:5; Rom. 6:1-11; 8:9-17; Gal. 19:20; 1 Pt. 2:9)*.

Formula: *Say, while pouring water (or dipping in water) on head of person to be baptised, 'N. I baptise you in the name of the Father, and of the Son and of the Holy Spirit.'*

2nd **Confirmation:** In this sacrament Christ gives us his Spirit with special strength to spread and defend the Faith. The bishop is the usual minister. *(Acts 1, 4-5, 8, 14-17, 10, 44-48. Ritual for sacraments.)*
The bishop (or priest) dips his right thumb in chrism and makes the sign of the cross on the forehead of the person as he says: 'N. be sealed with the Gift of the Holy Spirit.'

3rd **Eucharist:** Christ gives us this sacrament to make present for us his death, resurrection and ascension (Sacrifice of the Mass), to be the food of our souls in Holy Communion, and to remain with us in the Blessed Sacrament. *(Mt 26:26-29; Mk 14:22-25; Lk 22:15-20; Jn 6:34-58; 1 Cor 10:14-22, 11:17-30).*
Formula: Holy Mass — see words of Consecration in our section on the Mass. Holy Communion — 'The Body of Christ'. Response: 'Amen.'

4th **Penance:** When we go to Confession we have our sins committed after baptism forgiven by Christ through the priest. Christ gave us this gift on the day he rose from the dead. 'Penance obtains pardon from the mercy of God, and reunites the sinner with the Church which he has wounded by his sin.' *(VC2). (Jn 20:22-23; Mt 16:19, 18:18 — See our section on Going to Confession for Formula).*

5th **Anointing of the Sick:** Here Christ strengthens the body and soul of those in danger of death from serious illness. He increases grace in them, forgives their sins, remits punishment due to their sins and restores their health if it is good for them. 'By the anointing of the sick the Church commends the suffering to the Lord and asks them to contribute to welfare of the whole people of God by uniting themselves with the Passion of Christ.' (*VC2*). (*Mk 6:12-13; Js 5:14-16, cf. Mt 11:5, 10:1; Mk 16:18, 2:10-11; Lk 14:21; Rom 8:17*).

Formula: The priest anoints the sick person with oil first on the forehead, saying, 'Through this holy anointing may the Lord in his love and mercy help you with the grace of the Holy Spirit. Amen. Then on the hands, saying, 'May the Lord who frees you from sin save you and raise you up. Amen.'

6th **Holy Orders:** In this Christ gives a special share in his own priesthood (above that given to all Christians in Baptism), to bishops, priests and other Church ministers. The priest offers up the Sacrifice of the Mass, forgives sins in Confession, baptises, instructs, blesses. He is appointed to feed the Church in Christ's name with the word and grace of God.' (*VC2*). On that same first Holy Thursday when he instituted the sacrament of the Eucharist, Christ conferred priesthood on the apostles. 'Do this in memory of me'. (*Lk 22:14-20; Jn 20:22-23; Mt 10:1-4; Mk 3:13-19; Lk 6:12-16; Acts 6:1-6; 2 Cor 5:18-22; 1 Tim 5:22; 2 Tim 1:6; Tit 1:5.*)

Formula: For priesthood the bishop lays hands on the head of the candidate and says the words of consecration,

> ...*'Almighty Father, grant to this servant of yours the dignity of the priesthood. Renew within him the Spirit of holiness...'*

7th Matrimony: In this sacrament Christ joins the bridegroom and bride in a holy and unbreakable union and grants them graces to fulfil their duties faithfully. 'They have special importance in perpetuating the People of God. The family is the domestic Church.' (*VC 2*) (*Eph 5:25-32; Gen 1:27-28, 2:20-24; Mt 10:11-12; Rom 7:2-3; 1 Cor 7:10-11, 39*).

> *Formula: The couple administer the sacrament to each other. They declare their consent, 'I, N. take you N. as my wife (husband), for better, for worse, for richer, for poorer, in sickness and in health, till death do us part.'*

Fullness of Life — The sacraments are like fountains pouring divine life into us. Three of the sacraments, Baptism, Confirmation and the Eucharist are concerned with Christian initiation. 'The three sacraments of Christian initiation closely combine to bring the faithful to the full stature of Christ and to enable them to carry out the mission of the entire people of God in the Church and in the world.' (*Pope Paul VI, 1969*). The two sacraments of healing are Penance and Anointing of the Sick. The social sacraments are Holy Orders and Matrimony. The Church teaches that Baptism, Confirmation and Holy Orders imprint a permanent character or sign. They can be received only once.

8. What are sacramentals?

Sacramentals are objects and actions the Church uses to obtain from God various spiritual and temporal favours. Some types are Consecrations, Blessings, Exorcisms.

9. What are indulgences?

The Church believes that there are temporal punishments for sin. Sin brings punishment on us either in this life or in the next, unless we take punishment on ourselves by deeds of penance. Our penance is often incomplete, so the Church makes indulgences available for us. An indulgence is a remission before God of all (plenary indulgence) or part (partial indulgence) of the temporal punishment due to our sins already forgiven. To gain an indulgence, one must say the prayer or do the good act to which the Church attaches the indulgence.

10. What works of love help us grow spiritually in Christ?

Cf. Q.7 above. In questions 1-4 above we dealt with the necessity of showing our love of God in deeds rather than words. Conversion from sin is not enough, we must try to grow daily more like Jesus, the model and sources of all holiness. 'Instead, by speaking the truth in a spirit of love, we must grow up in every way to Christ, who is the head' *(Eph. 4:15)*. Prayer and the sacraments unite us to Christ while works of love show in practise how we live the life of love rooted in the Eucharist. Jesus shows this plainly in his narrative of the Last Judgment *(Mt. 25:31-46)*. 'You did it to me....' St Paul describes wonderfully the signs of true love in *1 Cor. 13:1-13,* and the effects of the spirit of love in *Gal. 5:22-26. See also the list of Spiritual and Corporal Works of Mercy in our appendix.* Christians should feel themselves obliged to promote the true common good. They should speak out against injustice and exploitation. They should reach out to help the needy, oppressed and forsaken. We are all children of God. Remember that Jesus said: 'Whenever you refused to help one of these least important ones, you refused to help me' *(Mt. 25:45).*

11. Have I a vocation in the Church?

Everyone has a vocation or calling to serve Christ in some way in the Church. Some do so as bishops, priests, deacons, religious priests, brothers, sisters. The majority serve as lay people. They work with Christ in the world by doing their everyday work well so as to develop themselves and the world; by helping the poor, the sick and the suffering because they see Christ in them; by improving family life; by helping young people; by trying to improve institutions, laws and customs. There is so much injustice in the world that all Christians should work together to end it. 'The apostolate of the laity derives from their Christian vocation and the Church can never be without it' *(VC 2).* Where am I? Have I found my vocation? *(cf. VC 2* on Apostolate of the Laity. *Acts 9:1-20; Gen. 2:15; 1 Cor. 10:31, 33; Eph. 6:8; 2 Thes. 3:6-13; Mt. 11:4-5; 25:31-46).*

Section 12
APPENDIX

'Gather the pieces left over!' (*John 6:12*)

1. **The Theological Virtues** are Faith, Hope and Charity.

2. **The chief mysteries of Faith**, which every Christian is bound to know, are the Unity and Trinity of God, who will render to every man according to his works, and the Incarnation, Death and Resurrection of our Saviour.

3. **The Cardinal Virtues** are Prudence, Justice, Fortitude and Temperance.

4. **The Seven Gifts of the Holy Spirit:**
Wisdom, Understanding, Right judgment, Courage, Knowledge, Reverence, Wonder and awe in God's presence.

5. **The twelve Fruits of the Holy Spirit** (*Gal 5:22-23; 1 Cor 13*): Love, Joy, Peace, Patience, Kindness, Goodness, Faithfulness, Humility, Faith, Modesty, Self-control, Chastity.

6. **The Seven Corporal Works of Mercy** (*Mt 25:31-46; Jas 2:1-26, 5:1-6*): To feed the hungry; to give drink to the thirsty; to clothe the naked; to shelter the homeless; to visit the sick; to visit the imprisoned; to bury the dead.

7. **The Seven Spiritual Works of Mercy:** To convert the sinner; to instruct the ignorant; to

counsel the doubtful; to comfort the sorrowful; to bear wrongs patiently; to forgive injuries; to pray for the living and the dead.

8. **True Happiness (Eight Beatitudes)** (*Mt 5:3-14; Lk 6:20-23*):
   1. Happy are those who know they are spiritually poor; the Kingdom of Heaven belongs to them!
   2. Happy are those who mourn; God will comfort them!
   3. Happy are those who are humble; they will receive what God has promised!
   4. Happy are those whose greatest desire is to do what God requires; God will satisfy them fully!
   5. Happy are those who are merciful to others; God will be merciful to them!
   6. Happy are the pure in heart; they will see God!
   7. Happy are those who work for peace; God will call them his children!
   8. Happy are those who are persecuted because they do what God requires; the Kingdom of Heaven belongs to them!

9. **The Seven Capital Sins:** Pride, Covetousness, Lust, Anger, Gluttony, Envy, Sloth.

10. **Every human being has certain natural essential rights.** They are: a right (1) to life; (2) to education and upbringing; (3) to liberty; (4) to work; (5) to rest and recreation; (6) to practise religion; (7) to follow conscience.

11. **The Four Last Things:** Death, Judgment, Heaven and Hell.

Section 13
RULE OF LIFE

How can I live my daily life on this Christian pilgrimage to the kingdom? Consider the following six attitudes and how you can express them practically each day.

1. Love life!

Life is a gift from God, each day is given to us in love. Jesus showed us how to protect endangered life and to heal the wounded. The Christian will try to make life worthy of human dignity and worth living for the greatest number of people. That means opposing all that kills life, such as murder and terrorism, euthanasia, abortion, suicide.

2. Be responsible!

A community flourishes when each individual acts responsibly by contributing individual talents, and expresses expectations and hopes. Christians are called so to act in family, school, neighbourhood, parish and the state. That means giving of one's talents and gifts to capacity, even for no financial reward.

3. Act in solidarity!

The Christian is not an individual but rather is bound to others. Many voluntary societies have been formed to come to the help of the poor, the sick and handicapped, the aged, the unemployed, prisoners, children and young people, and all in distress. It is not the function of the state to make all human suffering the business of officials only. Have I the patience and a caring heart to become involved?

4. Work hard and pray hard!
To balance work and leisure in our society can be a problem. If we have work we should be thankful for whatever contribution we can make to the development of society. But besides work there are also in life celebrations, games, friendships, walks, conversations, music and books, dreams and quiet times. Do I fritter away my time uselessly?

5. Pray at all times!
We can entrust our neighbours to the love of God. Through prayer for all the world we express our love. Daily prayer in some form feeds my Christian life. I can think of Mass and the Divine Office, of meditation, the Rosary, grace at meals, the Angelus, Bible reading or other spiritual literature.

6. Respect others!
My responsibility to share the goods of this world with others also demands my respect for property. I have to be detached, not always desirous of possessing. Possessing property implies social obligations, respecting with honesty other people's goods and private property, and their good name. Respect for the human body also means not to trivalise sexuality for commercial purposes. A Christian really does lead a different kind of life!

Parting words of Jesus our brother

'Do not let your hearts be troubled. Trust in God still, and trust in me. There are many rooms in my Father's home; if there were not, I should have told you. I am going now to prepare a place for you, and I shall return to take you with me' *(Jn. 14:1-2)*.

'I am the Way, the Truth and the Life. No one can come to the Father except through me' *(Jn.   14:5)*.

Why the Holy Spirit comes

No one can deny this most gracious and consolatory truth that the Holy Spirit has come; but why has he come? To supply Christ's absence, or to accomplish his presence? Surely to make him present. Let us not for a moment suppose that God the Holy Spirit comes in such sense that God the Son remains away. No, he has not so come that Christ does not come, but rather he comes that Christ may come in his coming. Through the Holy Spirit we have communion with the Father and the Son.

Cardinal Newman